CALM
THE
CHAOS

JOURNAL

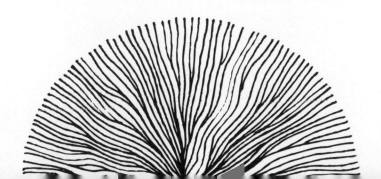

CALM

THE

CHAOS

JOURNAL

A Daily Practice for a More Peaceful Life

NICOLA RIES TAGGART

CHRONICLE BOOKS
SAN FRANCISCO

ISBN 978-1-4521-6995-8

Manufactured in China.

Design by Vanessa Dina
Typeset by Frank Brayton

10

Chronicle Books LLC
680 Second Street
San Francisco, California 94107
www.chroniclebooks.com

Welcome to your Calm the Chaos Journal!

You know that chaotic feeling that creeps up on you at the end of the day? You get into bed with the hopes of a good night's sleep, but as you try to drift into dreamland, your mind is overloaded and overwhelmed with the lists, challenges, and stress that come from being responsible for so much. If you could just calm the chaos in your mind, life would be sweeter and you would sleep better.

I created this journal for myself first, based on strategies and habits I have found to help me start and end my days in a more centered and focused way. I had tried all these different prompts for reflection and planning in different ways at different times, and I wanted a way to quickly and easily incorporate all of them into my daily routine.

After numerous conversations with clients of my life and leadership coaching practice, as well as friends and family, it was clear that I wasn't the only person with a full plate who could benefit from a simple structure and routine to help get centered and grounded at the start and end of each day. As I started sharing the journal with others, I was thrilled to hear that it resonated with them and had a positive impact beyond just my own experience.

I can't make your lists, challenges, and stress disappear. Only you can do that. But I can provide the *Calm the Chaos Journal* as a tool to help you manage the lists, tame the challenges, and decrease the stress so that you are able to feel healthier, happier, and more grateful, grounded, and peaceful.

My goal with this journal is to provide a simple yet effective way to help you feel more focused, centered, and sane by easily capturing an assessment of the day you are completing, as well as articulating your intention and focus for the following day.

May this serve as your practical and positive daily ritual—giving you the time and place to consciously calm the chaos and create a happier, healthier, more present and purposeful life!

To your success and sanity,

Nicola

NICOLA RIES TAGGART

How to Use the Calm the Chaos Journal

This journal was designed to support you in collecting your thoughts at the end of each day through the completion of one "Today" page and one "Tomorrow" page. And because I know you are busy, it's meant to be a quick practice that takes only ten minutes or so to complete before you go to bed and a couple of minutes to review in the morning (I keep mine on my bedside table).

The prompts in this journal were created around proven health and happiness habits and will help you reflect on and assess the positive things about the day you've completed, as well as support you in being intentional, focused, and prepared for the day ahead.

The health and happiness habits included here—taking care of yourself, performing acts of kindness toward others, articulating gratitude and appreciation, focusing attention and taking action on top priorities, setting positive intentions, and scanning your days for positive opportunities and ideas—are based on research that shows that consistent practice of them not only improves your own feelings of well-being and happiness, but also positively impacts those around you.

TODAY ENTRIES

Every "Today" page repeats the same prompts. I've included a brief explanation for each prompt below.

I took care of myself in the following ways:

This section is focused on the core ways we care for ourselves on a regular basis in order to feel present, productive, healthy, and happy. These are also the self-care practices that tend to be the hardest for people to incorporate regularly in their busy lives. Use this section to take stock of how you have taken care of yourself and to remind yourself that these practices are essential for maintaining overall physical, emotional, mental, and spiritual health and well-being.

An act of kindness I did for someone else was:

Altruism and happiness go hand in hand. This is not about doing everything for everyone else, at the expense of your own health. Rather, research shows us that when we do even small gestures for others, it improves our own mood—often triggering the release of feel-good hormones that have a direct impact on our positivity and productivity. Look for at least one small way to make a positive difference in someone else's life each day (e.g., send a note of appreciation, comment on a strength you witnessed from a colleague during a meeting, do that one thing for your spouse that they wouldn't expect you to do, buy the coffee for the person in line behind you, stop and help that person trying to get through the door, etc.).

My most memorable moment of the day was:
The idea of journaling on a regular basis at the end of a busy day can often feel overwhelming and unachievable, but if it's a quick task that becomes part of your nightly health and happiness ritual, it will become as routine as brushing your teeth! Capturing and documenting a memorable moment each day is an easy way to memorialize special memories in life, giving you something positive to look back on. The purpose of this section is to have you share a memory or moment from your day in one to three sentences, using just enough words to capture the essence of the memory.

I am grateful for:
Recording things you are thankful for on a regular basis
helps you focus on the positive things in life and regain
perspective after a challenging day. Use this section to
list up to five things—no matter how large or small—that
you are truly grateful for in your life. These things can
be different every day, or can repeat, depending on how
you're feeling in the moment. What matters most is that
you tap into that feeling of gratitude for a few moments
each day.

TOMORROW ENTRIES
The purpose of the "Tomorrow" prompts is to help get
you focused and act with intention the next day. For
added impact, take a few moments in the morning to
review what you wrote and remind yourself of your
intention and plan for the day ahead.

Unlike the "Today" entries, which repeat, the
prompts for the "Tomorrow" pages vary throughout the
journal. You'll find the following prompts rotating on the
"Tomorrow" pages:

My intention is
I will be guided by
My purpose is
I want to feel
My guiding mantra will be
Setting an intention is about being clear on your purpose and making an inner commitment to yourself about how you plan to be, show up, and operate in the world. In one sentence or a few short words, clarify how you plan to be, what you want to experience, or how you want to feel the next day. For example:

My intention/purpose is:
. . . *to be present with each person I am in contact with.*
. . . *to say yes only to things that I want to do.*
. . . *to let go of that which I cannot control and take action on that which I can.*

I will be guided by:
. . . *love, clarity, and kindness.*
. . . *choices that support simplicity and low stress.*
. . . *my top priorities and to-dos for the day.*

I want to feel:
... *calm, content, and clear.*
... *connected to what's most important to me.*
... *present and productive.*

My guiding mantra will be:
... *slow and steady wins the race.*
... *live what matters (and let the rest go).*
... *taking care of me allows me to better care for others.*

My top to-dos are
I will focus on
It would feel awesome to accomplish or complete
I will make time for
My top priorities are
The items you choose to add to your lists each day
should support your top priorities and have the biggest
impact on your life today (not necessarily be the tasks
that are the biggest, take the most time, or are life-
altering). Ask yourself, "If I get nothing else done today
except these things, what would feel good to accomplish? What needs to be accomplished to move my

goals forward in a positive way?" This is an opportunity to take that long, running to-do list of yours and choose three to five items that you will tackle tomorrow (because chaos comes when we try to take on more than is humanly possible in twenty-four hours).

Other thoughts, ideas, or notes:
What other thoughts are going through your head? Anything else on your mind you want to capture, remember, or let go of in order to have a better sleep tonight or a more positive, present, and productive day tomorrow? This is a blank space for you to make lists, journal, doodle, or sketch out your schedule for the next day. This is your space to use in whatever ways feel most constructive, supportive, and helpful in calming the chaos of your mind so you can feel more centered and less stressed before you turn off the light.

Something I need to let go of (and trust will work out):
Often the things that weigh on our minds, cause us stress, and keep us awake are things we cannot solve late at night when we should be sleeping. Write down the thing (or things) concerning you, send some good energy for it to work out as best it can, and let it go.

When I feel stressed, I will:
Feeling stressed is part of life. Knowing what you will do in the moment of stress to refocus on your intention is key to calming the chaos throughout your day. Take a moment to articulate what you will do when you feel stress so that when those feelings do arise you'll be prepared with a solution. A few ideas:

Go for a walk around the block.

Take ten deep breaths.

Call a good friend.

Listen to a song you love.

Remind yourself what your purpose/intention is for the day.

Send someone a message of appreciation.

A courageous conversation I need to have is:
I once heard someone say, "Stress is oftentimes conversations not had." So many times we have stress in our lives that could be greatly decreased or eliminated simply by having a courageous conversation. Think about something that is stressing you out and consider who you may need to talk to help decrease this stress.

What do you need to say? What's unresolved? What's unclear or confusing? What information or clarification do you need? The conversation may be uncomfortable, but keep in mind that there is a good chance the discomfort of having the talk will be less stressful than the longer-term discomfort you may feel if you don't have that conversation at all.

I want others to experience me as:
Every day we leave a legacy, whether we are conscious of it or not. Our legacy is based on the experience others have of us: the way we show up, the way we make them feel, the energy we bring into a room. Take a moment to be mindful of the way you want others to experience you. Let this help direct your attitude and behaviors as you go through your day.

I strongly encourage you to use this journal daily. The prompts are designed to be simple and achievable so that you can easily integrate this practice into your everyday life. Consistency is key when building new habits. If you commit to perform this journal ritual each day, you will feel a greater sense of inner peace, presence, and productivity in your life.

TODAY...

I took care of myself in the following ways:

○ Got adequate sleep: How much?

○ Moved my body: How?

○ Did something fun/pleasurable just for me: What?

○ Took time for reflection/meditation/prayer

○ Ate nutritious/nourishing food

○ Went outside for some fresh air

○ Other:

An act of kindness I did for someone else was:

My most memorable moment of the day was:

I am grateful for:

TOMORROW...

My intention is:

My top to-dos are:

Other thoughts, ideas, or notes:

TODAY...

I took care of myself in the following ways:

○ Got adequate sleep: How much?

○ Moved my body: How?

○ Did something fun/pleasurable just for me: What?

○ Took time for reflection/meditation/prayer

○ Ate nutritious/nourishing food

○ Went outside for some fresh air

○ Other:

An act of kindness I did for someone else was:

My most memorable moment of the day was:

I am grateful for:

TOMORROW...

I want to feel:

I will focus on:

Something I need to let go of (and trust will work out):

TODAY...

I took care of myself in the following ways:

○ Got adequate sleep: How much?

○ Moved my body: How?

○ Did something fun/pleasurable just for me: What?

○ Took time for reflection/meditation/prayer

○ Ate nutritious/nourishing food

○ Went outside for some fresh air

○ Other:

An act of kindness I did for someone else was:

My most memorable moment of the day was:

I am grateful for:

TOMORROW...

I will be guided by:

It would feel awesome to accomplish or complete:

When I feel stressed, I will:

TODAY...

I took care of myself in the following ways:

○ Got adequate sleep: How much?

○ Moved my body: How?

○ Did something fun/pleasurable just for me: What?

○ Took time for reflection/meditation/prayer

○ Ate nutritious/nourishing food

○ Went outside for some fresh air

○ Other:

An act of kindness I did for someone else was:

My most memorable moment of the day was:

I am grateful for:

TOMORROW...

My purpose is to:

I will make time for:

A courageous conversation I need to have is:

TODAY...

I took care of myself in the following ways:

○ Got adequate sleep: How much?

○ Moved my body: How?

○ Did something fun/pleasurable just for me: What?

○ Took time for reflection/meditation/prayer

○ Ate nutritious/nourishing food

○ Went outside for some fresh air

○ Other:

An act of kindness I did for someone else was:

My most memorable moment of the day was:

I am grateful for:

TOMORROW...

My guiding mantra will be:

My top priorities are:

I want others to experience me as:

TODAY...

I took care of myself in the following ways:

○ Got adequate sleep: How much?

○ Moved my body: How?

○ Did something fun/pleasurable just for me: What?

○ Took time for reflection/meditation/prayer

○ Ate nutritious/nourishing food

○ Went outside for some fresh air

○ Other:

An act of kindness I did for someone else was:

My most memorable moment of the day was:

I am grateful for:

TOMORROW...

My intention is:

My top to-dos are:

Other thoughts, ideas, or notes:

TODAY...

I took care of myself in the following ways:

○ Got adequate sleep: How much?

○ Moved my body: How?

○ Did something fun/pleasurable just for me: What?

○ Took time for reflection/meditation/prayer

○ Ate nutritious/nourishing food

○ Went outside for some fresh air

○ Other:

An act of kindness I did for someone else was:

My most memorable moment of the day was:

I am grateful for:

TOMORROW...

I want to feel:

I will focus on:

Something I need to let go of (and trust will work out):

TODAY...

I took care of myself in the following ways:

○ Got adequate sleep: How much?

○ Moved my body: How?

○ Did something fun/pleasurable just for me: What?

○ Took time for reflection/meditation/prayer

○ Ate nutritious/nourishing food

○ Went outside for some fresh air

○ Other:

An act of kindness I did for someone else was:

My most memorable moment of the day was:

I am grateful for:

TOMORROW...

I will be guided by:

It would feel awesome to accomplish or complete:

When I feel stressed, I will:

TODAY...

I took care of myself in the following ways:

○ Got adequate sleep: How much?

○ Moved my body: How?

○ Did something fun/pleasurable just for me: What?

○ Took time for reflection/meditation/prayer

○ Ate nutritious/nourishing food

○ Went outside for some fresh air

○ Other:

An act of kindness I did for someone else was:

My most memorable moment of the day was:

I am grateful for:

TOMORROW...

My purpose is to:

I will make time for:

A courageous conversation I need to have is:

TODAY...

I took care of myself in the following ways:

○ Got adequate sleep: How much?

○ Moved my body: How?

○ Did something fun/pleasurable just for me: What?

○ Took time for reflection/meditation/prayer

○ Ate nutritious/nourishing food

○ Went outside for some fresh air

○ Other:

An act of kindness I did for someone else was:

My most memorable moment of the day was:

I am grateful for:

TOMORROW...

My guiding mantra will be:

My top priorities are:

I want others to experience me as:

TODAY...

I took care of myself in the following ways:

○ Got adequate sleep: How much?

○ Moved my body: How?

○ Did something fun/pleasurable just for me: What?

○ Took time for reflection/meditation/prayer

○ Ate nutritious/nourishing food

○ Went outside for some fresh air

○ Other:

An act of kindness I did for someone else was:

My most memorable moment of the day was:

I am grateful for:

TOMORROW...

My intention is:

My top to-dos are:

Other thoughts, ideas, or notes:

TODAY...

I took care of myself in the following ways:

○ Got adequate sleep: How much?

○ Moved my body: How?

○ Did something fun/pleasurable just for me: What?

○ Took time for reflection/meditation/prayer

○ Ate nutritious/nourishing food

○ Went outside for some fresh air

○ Other:

An act of kindness I did for someone else was:

My most memorable moment of the day was:

I am grateful for:

TOMORROW...

I want to feel:

I will focus on:

Something I need to let go of (and trust will work out):

TODAY...

I took care of myself in the following ways:

○ Got adequate sleep: How much?

○ Moved my body: How?

○ Did something fun/pleasurable just for me: What?

○ Took time for reflection/meditation/prayer

○ Ate nutritious/nourishing food

○ Went outside for some fresh air

○ Other:

An act of kindness I did for someone else was:

My most memorable moment of the day was:

I am grateful for:

TOMORROW...

I will be guided by:

It would feel awesome to accomplish or complete:

When I feel stressed, I will:

TODAY...

I took care of myself in the following ways:

○ Got adequate sleep: How much?

○ Moved my body: How?

○ Did something fun/pleasurable just for me: What?

○ Took time for reflection/meditation/prayer

○ Ate nutritious/nourishing food

○ Went outside for some fresh air

○ Other:

An act of kindness I did for someone else was:

My most memorable moment of the day was:

I am grateful for:

TOMORROW...

My purpose is to:

I will make time for:

A courageous conversation I need to have is:

TODAY...

I took care of myself in the following ways:

○ Got adequate sleep: How much?

○ Moved my body: How?

○ Did something fun/pleasurable just for me: What?

○ Took time for reflection/meditation/prayer

○ Ate nutritious/nourishing food

○ Went outside for some fresh air

○ Other:

An act of kindness I did for someone else was:

My most memorable moment of the day was:

I am grateful for:

TOMORROW...

My guiding mantra will be:

My top priorities are:

I want others to experience me as:

TODAY...

I took care of myself in the following ways:

○ Got adequate sleep: How much?

○ Moved my body: How?

○ Did something fun/pleasurable just for me: What?

○ Took time for reflection/meditation/prayer

○ Ate nutritious/nourishing food

○ Went outside for some fresh air

○ Other:

An act of kindness I did for someone else was:

My most memorable moment of the day was:

I am grateful for:

TOMORROW...

My intention is:

My top to-dos are:

Other thoughts, ideas, or notes:

TODAY...

I took care of myself in the following ways:

○ Got adequate sleep: How much?

○ Moved my body: How?

○ Did something fun/pleasurable just for me: What?

○ Took time for reflection/meditation/prayer

○ Ate nutritious/nourishing food

○ Went outside for some fresh air

○ Other:

An act of kindness I did for someone else was:

My most memorable moment of the day was:

I am grateful for:

TOMORROW...

I want to feel:

I will focus on:

Something I need to let go of (and trust will work out):

TODAY...

I took care of myself in the following ways:

○ Got adequate sleep: How much?

○ Moved my body: How?

○ Did something fun/pleasurable just for me: What?

○ Took time for reflection/meditation/prayer

○ Ate nutritious/nourishing food

○ Went outside for some fresh air

○ Other:

An act of kindness I did for someone else was:

My most memorable moment of the day was:

I am grateful for:

TOMORROW...

I will be guided by:

It would feel awesome to accomplish or complete:

When I feel stressed, I will:

TODAY...

I took care of myself in the following ways:

○ Got adequate sleep: How much?

○ Moved my body: How?

○ Did something fun/pleasurable just for me: What?

○ Took time for reflection/meditation/prayer

○ Ate nutritious/nourishing food

○ Went outside for some fresh air

○ Other:

An act of kindness I did for someone else was:

My most memorable moment of the day was:

I am grateful for:

TOMORROW...

My purpose is to:

I will make time for:

A courageous conversation I need to have is:

TODAY...

I took care of myself in the following ways:

○ Got adequate sleep: How much?

○ Moved my body: How?

○ Did something fun/pleasurable just for me: What?

○ Took time for reflection/meditation/prayer

○ Ate nutritious/nourishing food

○ Went outside for some fresh air

○ Other:

An act of kindness I did for someone else was:

My most memorable moment of the day was:

I am grateful for:

TOMORROW...

My guiding mantra will be:

My top priorities are:

I want others to experience me as:

TODAY...

I took care of myself in the following ways:

○ Got adequate sleep: How much?

○ Moved my body: How?

○ Did something fun/pleasurable just for me: What?

○ Took time for reflection/meditation/prayer

○ Ate nutritious/nourishing food

○ Went outside for some fresh air

○ Other:

An act of kindness I did for someone else was:

My most memorable moment of the day was:

I am grateful for:

TOMORROW...

My intention is:

My top to-dos are:

Other thoughts, ideas, or notes:

TODAY...

I took care of myself in the following ways:

○ Got adequate sleep: How much?

○ Moved my body: How?

○ Did something fun/pleasurable just for me: What?

○ Took time for reflection/meditation/prayer

○ Ate nutritious/nourishing food

○ Went outside for some fresh air

○ Other:

An act of kindness I did for someone else was:

My most memorable moment of the day was:

I am grateful for:

TOMORROW...

I want to feel:

I will focus on:

Something I need to let go of (and trust will work out):

TODAY...

I took care of myself in the following ways:

◯ Got adequate sleep: How much?

◯ Moved my body: How?

◯ Did something fun/pleasurable just for me: What?

◯ Took time for reflection/meditation/prayer

◯ Ate nutritious/nourishing food

◯ Went outside for some fresh air

◯ Other:

An act of kindness I did for someone else was:

My most memorable moment of the day was:

I am grateful for:

TOMORROW...

I will be guided by:

It would feel awesome to accomplish or complete:

When I feel stressed, I will:

TODAY...

I took care of myself in the following ways:

○ Got adequate sleep: How much?

○ Moved my body: How?

○ Did something fun/pleasurable just for me: What?

○ Took time for reflection/meditation/prayer

○ Ate nutritious/nourishing food

○ Went outside for some fresh air

○ Other:

An act of kindness I did for someone else was:

My most memorable moment of the day was:

I am grateful for:

TOMORROW...

My purpose is to:

I will make time for:

A courageous conversation I need to have is:

TODAY...

I took care of myself in the following ways:

○ Got adequate sleep: How much?

○ Moved my body: How?

○ Did something fun/pleasurable just for me: What?

○ Took time for reflection/meditation/prayer

○ Ate nutritious/nourishing food

○ Went outside for some fresh air

○ Other:

An act of kindness I did for someone else was:

My most memorable moment of the day was:

I am grateful for:

TOMORROW...

My guiding mantra will be:

My top priorities are:

I want others to experience me as:

TODAY...

I took care of myself in the following ways:

○ Got adequate sleep: How much?

○ Moved my body: How?

○ Did something fun/pleasurable just for me: What?

○ Took time for reflection/meditation/prayer

○ Ate nutritious/nourishing food

○ Went outside for some fresh air

○ Other:

An act of kindness I did for someone else was:

My most memorable moment of the day was:

I am grateful for:

TOMORROW...

My intention is:

My top to-dos are:

Other thoughts, ideas, or notes:

TODAY...

I took care of myself in the following ways:

◯ Got adequate sleep: How much?

◯ Moved my body: How?

◯ Did something fun/pleasurable just for me: What?

◯ Took time for reflection/meditation/prayer

◯ Ate nutritious/nourishing food

◯ Went outside for some fresh air

◯ Other:

An act of kindness I did for someone else was:

My most memorable moment of the day was:

I am grateful for:

TOMORROW...

I want to feel:

I will focus on:

Something I need to let go of (and trust will work out):

TODAY...

I took care of myself in the following ways:

○ Got adequate sleep: How much?

○ Moved my body: How?

○ Did something fun/pleasurable just for me: What?

○ Took time for reflection/meditation/prayer

○ Ate nutritious/nourishing food

○ Went outside for some fresh air

○ Other:

An act of kindness I did for someone else was:

My most memorable moment of the day was:

I am grateful for:

TOMORROW...

I will be guided by:

It would feel awesome to accomplish or complete:

When I feel stressed, I will:

TODAY...

I took care of myself in the following ways:

○ Got adequate sleep: How much?

○ Moved my body: How?

○ Did something fun/pleasurable just for me: What?

○ Took time for reflection/meditation/prayer

○ Ate nutritious/nourishing food

○ Went outside for some fresh air

○ Other:

An act of kindness I did for someone else was:

My most memorable moment of the day was:

I am grateful for:

TOMORROW...

My purpose is to:

I will make time for:

A courageous conversation I need to have is:

TODAY...

I took care of myself in the following ways:

○ Got adequate sleep: How much?

○ Moved my body: How?

○ Did something fun/pleasurable just for me: What?

○ Took time for reflection/meditation/prayer

○ Ate nutritious/nourishing food

○ Went outside for some fresh air

○ Other:

An act of kindness I did for someone else was:

My most memorable moment of the day was:

I am grateful for:

TOMORROW...

My guiding mantra will be:

My top priorities are:

I want others to experience me as:

TODAY...

I took care of myself in the following ways:

○ Got adequate sleep: How much?

○ Moved my body: How?

○ Did something fun/pleasurable just for me: What?

○ Took time for reflection/meditation/prayer

○ Ate nutritious/nourishing food

○ Went outside for some fresh air

○ Other:

An act of kindness I did for someone else was:

My most memorable moment of the day was:

I am grateful for:

TOMORROW...

My intention is:

My top to-dos are:

Other thoughts, ideas, or notes:

TODAY...

I took care of myself in the following ways:

○ Got adequate sleep: How much?

○ Moved my body: How?

○ Did something fun/pleasurable just for me: What?

○ Took time for reflection/meditation/prayer

○ Ate nutritious/nourishing food

○ Went outside for some fresh air

○ Other:

An act of kindness I did for someone else was:

My most memorable moment of the day was:

I am grateful for:

TOMORROW...

I want to feel:

I will focus on:

Something I need to let go of (and trust will work out):

TODAY...

I took care of myself in the following ways:

○ Got adequate sleep: How much?

○ Moved my body: How?

○ Did something fun/pleasurable just for me: What?

○ Took time for reflection/meditation/prayer

○ Ate nutritious/nourishing food

○ Went outside for some fresh air

○ Other:

An act of kindness I did for someone else was:

My most memorable moment of the day was:

I am grateful for:

TOMORROW...

I will be guided by:

It would feel awesome to accomplish or complete:

When I feel stressed, I will:

TODAY...

I took care of myself in the following ways:

○ Got adequate sleep: How much?

○ Moved my body: How?

○ Did something fun/pleasurable just for me: What?

○ Took time for reflection/meditation/prayer

○ Ate nutritious/nourishing food

○ Went outside for some fresh air

○ Other:

An act of kindness I did for someone else was:

My most memorable moment of the day was:

I am grateful for:

TOMORROW...

My purpose is to:

I will make time for:

A courageous conversation I need to have is:

TODAY...

I took care of myself in the following ways:

○ Got adequate sleep: How much?

○ Moved my body: How?

○ Did something fun/pleasurable just for me: What?

○ Took time for reflection/meditation/prayer

○ Ate nutritious/nourishing food

○ Went outside for some fresh air

○ Other:

An act of kindness I did for someone else was:

My most memorable moment of the day was:

I am grateful for:

TOMORROW...

My guiding mantra will be:

My top priorities are:

I want others to experience me as:

TODAY...

I took care of myself in the following ways:

○ Got adequate sleep: How much?

○ Moved my body: How?

○ Did something fun/pleasurable just for me: What?

○ Took time for reflection/meditation/prayer

○ Ate nutritious/nourishing food

○ Went outside for some fresh air

○ Other:

An act of kindness I did for someone else was:

My most memorable moment of the day was:

I am grateful for:

TOMORROW...

My intention is:

My top to-dos are:

Other thoughts, ideas, or notes:

TODAY...

I took care of myself in the following ways:

◯ Got adequate sleep: How much?

◯ Moved my body: How?

◯ Did something fun/pleasurable just for me: What?

◯ Took time for reflection/meditation/prayer

◯ Ate nutritious/nourishing food

◯ Went outside for some fresh air

◯ Other:

An act of kindness I did for someone else was:

My most memorable moment of the day was:

I am grateful for:

TOMORROW...

I want to feel:

I will focus on:

Something I need to let go of (and trust will work out):

TODAY...

I took care of myself in the following ways:

○ Got adequate sleep: How much?

○ Moved my body: How?

○ Did something fun/pleasurable just for me: What?

○ Took time for reflection/meditation/prayer

○ Ate nutritious/nourishing food

○ Went outside for some fresh air

○ Other:

An act of kindness I did for someone else was:

My most memorable moment of the day was:

I am grateful for:

TOMORROW...

I will be guided by:

It would feel awesome to accomplish or complete:

When I feel stressed, I will:

TODAY...

I took care of myself in the following ways:

○ Got adequate sleep: How much?

○ Moved my body: How?

○ Did something fun/pleasurable just for me: What?

○ Took time for reflection/meditation/prayer

○ Ate nutritious/nourishing food

○ Went outside for some fresh air

○ Other:

An act of kindness I did for someone else was:

My most memorable moment of the day was:

I am grateful for:

TOMORROW...

My purpose is to:

I will make time for:

A courageous conversation I need to have is:

TODAY...

I took care of myself in the following ways:

○ Got adequate sleep: How much?

○ Moved my body: How?

○ Did something fun/pleasurable just for me: What?

○ Took time for reflection/meditation/prayer

○ Ate nutritious/nourishing food

○ Went outside for some fresh air

○ Other:

An act of kindness I did for someone else was:

My most memorable moment of the day was:

I am grateful for:

TOMORROW...

My guiding mantra will be:

My top priorities are:

I want others to experience me as:

TODAY...

I took care of myself in the following ways:

○ Got adequate sleep: How much?

○ Moved my body: How?

○ Did something fun/pleasurable just for me: What?

○ Took time for reflection/meditation/prayer

○ Ate nutritious/nourishing food

○ Went outside for some fresh air

○ Other:

An act of kindness I did for someone else was:

My most memorable moment of the day was:

I am grateful for:

TOMORROW...

My intention is:

My top to-dos are:

Other thoughts, ideas, or notes:

TODAY...

I took care of myself in the following ways:

○ Got adequate sleep: How much?

○ Moved my body: How?

○ Did something fun/pleasurable just for me: What?

○ Took time for reflection/meditation/prayer

○ Ate nutritious/nourishing food

○ Went outside for some fresh air

○ Other:

An act of kindness I did for someone else was:

My most memorable moment of the day was:

I am grateful for:

TOMORROW...

I want to feel:

I will focus on:

Something I need to let go of (and trust will work out):

TODAY...

I took care of myself in the following ways:

◯ Got adequate sleep: How much?

◯ Moved my body: How?

◯ Did something fun/pleasurable just for me: What?

◯ Took time for reflection/meditation/prayer

◯ Ate nutritious/nourishing food

◯ Went outside for some fresh air

◯ Other:

An act of kindness I did for someone else was:

My most memorable moment of the day was:

I am grateful for:

TOMORROW...

I will be guided by:

It would feel awesome to accomplish or complete:

When I feel stressed, I will:

TODAY...

I took care of myself in the following ways:

○ Got adequate sleep: How much?

○ Moved my body: How?

○ Did something fun/pleasurable just for me: What?

○ Took time for reflection/meditation/prayer

○ Ate nutritious/nourishing food

○ Went outside for some fresh air

○ Other:

An act of kindness I did for someone else was:

My most memorable moment of the day was:

I am grateful for:

TOMORROW...

My purpose is to:

I will make time for:

A courageous conversation I need to have is:

TODAY...

I took care of myself in the following ways:

○ Got adequate sleep: How much?

○ Moved my body: How?

○ Did something fun/pleasurable just for me: What?

○ Took time for reflection/meditation/prayer

○ Ate nutritious/nourishing food

○ Went outside for some fresh air

○ Other:

An act of kindness I did for someone else was:

My most memorable moment of the day was:

I am grateful for:

TOMORROW...

My guiding mantra will be:

My top priorities are:

I want others to experience me as:

TODAY...

I took care of myself in the following ways:

○ Got adequate sleep: How much?

○ Moved my body: How?

○ Did something fun/pleasurable just for me: What?

○ Took time for reflection/meditation/prayer

○ Ate nutritious/nourishing food

○ Went outside for some fresh air

○ Other:

An act of kindness I did for someone else was:

My most memorable moment of the day was:

I am grateful for:

TOMORROW...

My intention is:

My top to-dos are:

Other thoughts, ideas, or notes:

TODAY...

I took care of myself in the following ways:

○ Got adequate sleep: How much?

○ Moved my body: How?

○ Did something fun/pleasurable just for me: What?

○ Took time for reflection/meditation/prayer

○ Ate nutritious/nourishing food

○ Went outside for some fresh air

○ Other:

An act of kindness I did for someone else was:

My most memorable moment of the day was:

I am grateful for:

TOMORROW...

I want to feel:

I will focus on:

Something I need to let go of (and trust will work out):

TODAY...

I took care of myself in the following ways:

○ Got adequate sleep: How much?

○ Moved my body: How?

○ Did something fun/pleasurable just for me: What?

○ Took time for reflection/meditation/prayer

○ Ate nutritious/nourishing food

○ Went outside for some fresh air

○ Other:

An act of kindness I did for someone else was:

My most memorable moment of the day was:

I am grateful for:

TOMORROW...

I will be guided by:

It would feel awesome to accomplish or complete:

When I feel stressed, I will:

TODAY...

I took care of myself in the following ways:

○ Got adequate sleep: How much?

○ Moved my body: How?

○ Did something fun/pleasurable just for me: What?

○ Took time for reflection/meditation/prayer

○ Ate nutritious/nourishing food

○ Went outside for some fresh air

○ Other:

An act of kindness I did for someone else was:

My most memorable moment of the day was:

I am grateful for:

TOMORROW...

My purpose is to:

I will make time for:

A courageous conversation I need to have is:

TODAY...

I took care of myself in the following ways:

◯ Got adequate sleep: How much?

◯ Moved my body: How?

◯ Did something fun/pleasurable just for me: What?

◯ Took time for reflection/meditation/prayer

◯ Ate nutritious/nourishing food

◯ Went outside for some fresh air

◯ Other:

An act of kindness I did for someone else was:

My most memorable moment of the day was:

I am grateful for:

TOMORROW...

My guiding mantra will be:

My top priorities are:

I want others to experience me as:

TODAY...

I took care of myself in the following ways:

○ Got adequate sleep: How much?

○ Moved my body: How?

○ Did something fun/pleasurable just for me: What?

○ Took time for reflection/meditation/prayer

○ Ate nutritious/nourishing food

○ Went outside for some fresh air

○ Other:

An act of kindness I did for someone else was:

My most memorable moment of the day was:

I am grateful for:

TOMORROW...

My intention is:

My top to-dos are:

Other thoughts, ideas, or notes:

TODAY...

I took care of myself in the following ways:

○ Got adequate sleep: How much?

○ Moved my body: How?

○ Did something fun/pleasurable just for me: What?

○ Took time for reflection/meditation/prayer

○ Ate nutritious/nourishing food

○ Went outside for some fresh air

○ Other:

An act of kindness I did for someone else was:

My most memorable moment of the day was:

I am grateful for:

TOMORROW...

I want to feel:

I will focus on:

Something I need to let go of (and trust will work out):

TODAY...

I took care of myself in the following ways:

○ Got adequate sleep: How much?

○ Moved my body: How?

○ Did something fun/pleasurable just for me: What?

○ Took time for reflection/meditation/prayer

○ Ate nutritious/nourishing food

○ Went outside for some fresh air

○ Other:

An act of kindness I did for someone else was:

My most memorable moment of the day was:

I am grateful for:

TOMORROW...

I will be guided by:

It would feel awesome to accomplish or complete:

When I feel stressed, I will:

TODAY...

I took care of myself in the following ways:

○ Got adequate sleep: How much?

○ Moved my body: How?

○ Did something fun/pleasurable just for me: What?

○ Took time for reflection/meditation/prayer

○ Ate nutritious/nourishing food

○ Went outside for some fresh air

○ Other:

An act of kindness I did for someone else was:

My most memorable moment of the day was:

I am grateful for:

TOMORROW...

My purpose is to:

I will make time for:

A courageous conversation I need to have is:

TODAY...

I took care of myself in the following ways:

○ Got adequate sleep: How much?

○ Moved my body: How?

○ Did something fun/pleasurable just for me: What?

○ Took time for reflection/meditation/prayer

○ Ate nutritious/nourishing food

○ Went outside for some fresh air

○ Other:

An act of kindness I did for someone else was:

My most memorable moment of the day was:

I am grateful for:

TOMORROW...

My guiding mantra will be:

My top priorities are:

I want others to experience me as:

TODAY...

I took care of myself in the following ways:

○ Got adequate sleep: How much?

○ Moved my body: How?

○ Did something fun/pleasurable just for me: What?

○ Took time for reflection/meditation/prayer

○ Ate nutritious/nourishing food

○ Went outside for some fresh air

○ Other:

An act of kindness I did for someone else was:

My most memorable moment of the day was:

I am grateful for:

TOMORROW...

My intention is:

My top to-dos are:

Other thoughts, ideas, or notes:

TODAY...

I took care of myself in the following ways:

○ Got adequate sleep: How much?

○ Moved my body: How?

○ Did something fun/pleasurable just for me: What?

○ Took time for reflection/meditation/prayer

○ Ate nutritious/nourishing food

○ Went outside for some fresh air

○ Other:

An act of kindness I did for someone else was:

My most memorable moment of the day was:

I am grateful for:

TOMORROW...

I want to feel:

I will focus on:

Something I need to let go of (and trust will work out):

TODAY...

I took care of myself in the following ways:

○ Got adequate sleep: How much?

○ Moved my body: How?

○ Did something fun/pleasurable just for me: What?

○ Took time for reflection/meditation/prayer

○ Ate nutritious/nourishing food

○ Went outside for some fresh air

○ Other:

An act of kindness I did for someone else was:

My most memorable moment of the day was:

I am grateful for:

TOMORROW...

I will be guided by:

It would feel awesome to accomplish or complete:

When I feel stressed, I will:

TODAY...

I took care of myself in the following ways:

○ Got adequate sleep: How much?

○ Moved my body: How?

○ Did something fun/pleasurable just for me: What?

○ Took time for reflection/meditation/prayer

○ Ate nutritious/nourishing food

○ Went outside for some fresh air

○ Other:

An act of kindness I did for someone else was:

My most memorable moment of the day was:

I am grateful for:

TOMORROW...

My purpose is to:

I will make time for:

A courageous conversation I need to have is:

TODAY...

I took care of myself in the following ways:

○ Got adequate sleep: How much?

○ Moved my body: How?

○ Did something fun/pleasurable just for me: What?

○ Took time for reflection/meditation/prayer

○ Ate nutritious/nourishing food

○ Went outside for some fresh air

○ Other:

An act of kindness I did for someone else was:

My most memorable moment of the day was:

I am grateful for:

TOMORROW...

My guiding mantra will be:

My top priorities are:

I want others to experience me as:

TODAY...

I took care of myself in the following ways:

○ Got adequate sleep: How much?

○ Moved my body: How?

○ Did something fun/pleasurable just for me: What?

○ Took time for reflection/meditation/prayer

○ Ate nutritious/nourishing food

○ Went outside for some fresh air

○ Other:

An act of kindness I did for someone else was:

My most memorable moment of the day was:

I am grateful for:

TOMORROW...

My intention is:

My top to-dos are:

Other thoughts, ideas, or notes:

Nicola Ries Taggart is a life and leadership success strategist, speaker, workshop facilitator, and coach. She has devoted her career to helping individuals, couples, and teams take ownership of their lives, choices, and happiness. She lives in Alameda, California, with her family. To learn more about Nicola and her work, visit **www.nicolataggart.com.**